The Year of the Poet VIII

April 2021

The Poetry Posse

inner child press, ltd.

The Poetry Posse 2021

Gail Weston Shazor
Shareef Abdur Rasheed
Teresa E. Gallion
hülya n. yılmaz
Kimberly Burnham
Tzemin Ition Tsai
Elizabeth Esguerra Castillo
Jackie Davis Allen
Joe Paire
Caroline 'Ceri' Nazareno
Ashok K. Bhargava
Alicja Maria Kuberska
Swapna Behera
Albert 'Infinite' Carrasco
Eliza Segiet
William S. Peters, Sr.

~ * ~

In order to maintain each poet's authentic voice, this volume has not undergone the scrutiny of editing. Please take time to indulge each contributor for their own creativity and aspirations to convey their uniqueness.

hülya n. yılmaz, Ph.D.
Director of Editing ~
Inner Child Press International

General Information

The Year of the Poet VIII
April 2021 Edition

The Poetry Posse

1st Edition : 2021

This Publishing is protected under Copyright Law as a "Collection". All rights for all submissions are retained by the Individual Author and or Artist. No part of this Publishing may be Reproduced, Transferred in any manner without the prior **WRITTEN CONSENT** of the "Material Owners" or its Representative Inner Child Press. Any such violation infringes upon the Creative and Intellectual Property of the Owner pursuant to International and Federal Copyright Laws. Any queries pertaining to this "Collection" should be addressed to Publisher of Record.

Publisher Information
1st Edition : Inner Child Press
intouch@innerchildpress.com
www.innerchildpress.com

This Collection is protected under U.S. and International Copyright Laws

Copyright © 2021 : The Poetry Posse

ISBN-13 : 978-1-952081-47-7 (inner child press, ltd.)

$ 12.99

WHAT WOULD
LIFE
BE WITHOUT
A LITTLE
POETRY?

Dedication

This Book is dedicated to

Humanity, Peace & Poetry

the Power of the Pen

can effectuate change!

&

The Poetry Posse

past, present & future

our Patrons and Readers

the Spirit of our Everlasting Muse

In the darkness of my life
I heard the music
I danced...
and the Light appeared
and I dance

Janet P. Caldwell

Table of Contents

Foreword ix
Preface xi
The Feature xiii

The Poetry Posse

Gail Weston Shazor	1
Alicja Maria Kuberska	9
Jackie Davis Allen	15
Tezmin Ition Tsai	21
Shareef Abdur – Rasheed	27
Kimberly Burnham	33
Elizabeth Esguerra Castillo	39
Joe Paire	45
hülya n. yılmaz	51
Teresa E. Gallion	57
Ashok K. Bhargava	63
Caroline Nazareno-Gabis	69

Table of Contents . . . *continued*

Swapna Behera	75
Albert Carassco	83
Eliza Segiet	89
William S. Peters, Sr.	95

April's Featured Poets — 105

Katarzyna Brus-Sawczuk	107
Anwesha Paul	113
Rozalia Aleksandrova	119
Shahid Abbas	125

Inner Child News — 135

Other Anthological Works — 165

Foreword

Pablo O'Higgins

The Poetry Posse remembers the American-Mexican muralist whose works had influenced powerful instrument in the global context of defeating fascism and other forces of oppression.

Pablo O'Higgins was born in Utah, grew in California and flourished in Mexico.

He started his artistic training at the School of Fine Arts in San Diego, then moved to Mexico when he was 20.

O' Higgins joined the circle of anti-fascist League of Revolutionary Artists and Writers (Liga de Escritores y Artistas Revolucionarias, or LEAR) including the master muralist Diego Rivera, José Clemente Orozco, and David Alfaro Siquerios, and later, he became Rivera's assistant.

His *obras* expressed dramatic and monumental realism, which he adopted in depicting images of labor and local inhabitants. His works had intriguing history.

He is considered as one of the most important muralists of its "second generation" of mural painters.

Sources stated that O'Higgins became politically active in the post-revolution art movement in Mexico. He was the only non-native to be included in the historic 1940 exhibition at the New York Museum of Modern Art, "Twenty Centuries of Mexican Art.

O'Higgins played a significant role in Mexican-US connections, thus, his contributions to the national arts and education had paved way to get an honorary Mexican citizenship in 1961.

His sixty-foot long mural strong anti-racist, anti-discriminatory, politically rebellious mural entitled **Ship Scalers Union Hall** in Seattle is installed in Kane Hall, University of Washington, Seattle. The mural represents Seattle's Ship Scalers Union's (SSU) history in social politics.

Pablo O'Higgins murals had etched inspirations in history of struggle for social change.

Caroline Nazareno 'Ceri Naz' Gabis

Preface

Dear Family and Friends,

So, here we are, beginning our eighth year of monthly publication of *The Year of the Poet*. Amazing how much effort has been given by all the poets, to include the various members of *The Poetry Posse* and all the wonderful featured poets from all over our world. For myself, it has been and continues to be a great honor to be a part of this wonderful cooperative effort.

Last year, 2020 has been challenging for many of us throughout the year. We at *Inner Child Press International* were busy. We envisioned our role where the arts meet humanity to continue doing what we were good at . . . publishing. We managed to not only produce and publish this series, *The Year of the Poet* each month, but we were also very proactive in the arena of human and social consciousness. We were able to produce several other anthologies to include: World Healing, World Peace 2020; CORONA . . . social distancing; The Heart of a Poet; W.A.R. . . . we are revolution; Poetry, the Best of 2020. Going forward, we are seeking to invest in the same or greater effort towards contributing to a 'conscious humanity'. We, poets and writers do have something to say about it all, and we intend to do so in any and every way we can. So stay tuned . . .

Bill

William S. Peters, Sr.

Publisher
Inner Child Press International

www.innerchildpress.com

PS

Do Not forget about the World Healing, World Peace Poetry initiative for 2022. Mark your calendars. Submissions will be opening . . .
September 1st 2021

Past volumes are vailable here

www.worldhealingworldpeacepoetry.com

**For Free Downloads of Previous Issues of
The Year of the Poet**

www.innerchildpress.com/the-year-of-the-poet

Pablo O'Higgins

April 2021

Pablo O'Higgins studied art at the School of Fine Arts in San Diego and developed an affinity with revolutionary Mexican artists. An assistant to Diego Rivera, a lifetime friend, and a mentor, O'Higgins created many images of labor and local inhabitants. He became politically active in the post-revolution art movement in Mexico.

https://www.historylink.org/Content/Media/Photos/Small/PabloOHigginsMuralKaneHallSeattleMexicanAmerican.jpg
https://en.wikipedia.org/wiki/Pablo_O%27Higgins

Pablo O'Higgins dedicated his artwork to "the struggle against racial discrimination and transnational perspectives."

https://www.historylink.org/Content/Media/Photos/Small/PabloOHigginsMuralKaneHallSeattleMexicanAmerican02.jpg

Poets . . .
sowing seeds in the
Conscious Garden of Life,
that those who have yet to come
may enjoy the Flowers.

Poets, Writers . . . know that we are the enchanting magicians that nourishes the seeds of dreams and thoughts . . . it is our words that entice the hearts and minds of others to believe there is something grand about the possibilities that life has to offer and our words tease it forth into action . . . for you are the Poet, the Writer to whom the Gift of Words has been entrusted . . .

~ wsp

Poetry succeeds where instruction fails.

~ wsp

Gail Weston Shazor

Gail Weston Shazor

This is a creative promise ~ my pen will speak to and for the world. Enamored with letters and respectful of their power, I have been writing for most of my life. A mother, daughter, sister and grandmother I give what I have been given, greatfilledly.

Author of . . .

"An Overstanding of an Imperfect Love"
&
Notes from the Blue Roof

Lies My Grandfathers Told Me

available at Inner Child Press.

www.facebook.com/gailwestonshazor
www.innerchildpress.com/gail-weston-shazor
navypoet1@gmail.com

Gail Iskulani Weston Shazor

What's in a blood name?
We are everything
All at once
Irish and Latin
Choctaw and Caucasian
Melungeon
African American
Negro
Black
Mixed
And we choose
To be even more
Sometimes changing our names
To solidify
A new world
But not the columbused one
In which we live
We dream of being free
To be FREE

Smiles

I think it's your smile
So much more
Than lips
The way it sparkles
With
Very
New
Secrets
Extending the corners upwards
And sparing the leftover glimmers
For waiting eyes
Even they need to
Catch up
Meet up
Match up
To the sensuality
Of the humor cloaked within
Exuding
Yes. I think it's your smile
That I long to try out
Just to see if
It is
My size
My flavor
My silence
I become pleased
When you share it with me
But I am lost
When I am the cause

At the Crosswords

"And still keepin up wit they family
Exactly how many days we got lastin' while you laughin'
we passin'
Passin' away"

On the block
Passing time away
Me and my boys
Laughing and drinking and smoking
We been on the truck all day
Chasing that dollar bill, y'all
Cuz this woman, she want thangs
And my kids, they need thangs
And my momma, she deserves thangs
All they got is me
The only daddy left
The money don't come fast enough
So I gotta do what I gotta do
Until I can't no more
It used to be just a bag or two
And that was easy
Now folks be calling my name
Round the way
I gotta have a crew to watch my back
But now they backs
Facing the stars
And I know I might be next
That's them VI streets tho
I kissed my momma today
And hugged all my chirren
Because today might be that day
That I won't be coming home

And I meet my daddy at the crossroad
They say the devil went down to Georgia
But I saw him last week
And he winked at me

"And I ask the good lord why
He sigh, he told me we live to die
Whats up with that murder y'all?"

Gail Weston Shazor

Alicja Maria Kuberska

Alicja Maria Kuberska

Alicja Maria Kuberska – awarded Polish poetess, novelist, journalist, editor.

She is a member of the Polish Writers Associations in Warsaw, Poland and IWA Bogdani, Albania. She is also a member of directors' board of Soflay Literature Foundation, Our Poetry Archive (India) and Cultural Ambassador for Poland (Inner Child Press, USA)

Her poems have been published in numerous anthologies and magazines in : Poland, Czech Republic, Slovakia, Hungary,Ukraina, Belgium, Bulgaria, Albania, Spain, the UK, Italy, the USA, Canada, the UK, Argentina, Chile, Peru, Israel, Turkey, India, Uzbekistan, South Korea, Taiwan, China, Australia, South Africa, Zambia, Nigeria

She received two medals - the Nosside UNESCO Competition in Italy (2015) and European Academy of Science Arts and Letters in France (2017). Ahe also received a reward of international literary competition in Italy „ Tra le parole e 'elfinito" (2018). She was announced a poet of the 2017 year by Soflay Literature Foundation (2018).She also received : Bolesław Prus Prize Poland (2019), Culture Animator Poland (2019) and first prize Premio Internazionale di Poesia Poseidonia- Paestrum Italy (2019).

Streets say
Poem dedicated to Pablo O'Higgins

Listen to the voices of the street
- Soft murmurs of dissatisfaction
And shouted out revolutionary slogans

The mood of the city changes quickly
When the charming cafes go silent
And the main arteries buzz loudly.

There is a growing anxiety in the air
The apparent order breaks down,
And silent anger is as tornadoes

Then the street boils, bubbles and soars
Like a mad river during a flood
 -Shoulder by shoulder, word by word.

Listen to the voices of the street
Know their destructive force
Hear a voice of a simple man

Farewell to Medusa*

Goodbye our golden-winged sister .

You died unprotected in your sleep.
There is a stone dream in your eyes
And a frozen grimace of pain on your lips.

The sickle cut the thread of your life .
You were like a stalk and he mutilated you.
Sorry my dear - we didn't avenge you.

The murderer disappeared unnoticed.
He hid in fluffy clouds
And behind the rays of the sun.

Wish you could see
How calm the ocean is today.
Despair lasts in the silence of the depths.

*The ancient Greek myth. Medusa, the youngest sister of Gorgon, beloved of Poseidon, was killed by Perseus, who cut her head.

Untolerant people

Sword and Bible
Kalashnikov and Quran
should not fit together
like love and hatred

There are people ,
who know everything the best
They know
God's thoughts and plans
 and they are infallible.

These people are able
 to break the stone tablets
and build a road with them
leading straight
   ... to a hellish paradise.

Jackie Davis Allen

Jackie Davis Allen

Jackie Davis Allen, otherwise known as Jacqueline D. Allen or Jackie Allen, grew up in the Cumberland Mountains of Appalachia. As the next eldest daughter of a coal miner father and a stay at home mother, she was the first in her family to attend and graduate from college. Her siblings, in their own right, are accomplished, though she is the only one, to date, that has discovered the gift of writing.

Graduating from Radford University, with a Bachelors of Science degree in Early Education, she taught in both public and private schools. For over a decade she taught private art classes to children both in her home and at a local Art and Framing Shop where she also sold her original soft sculptured Victorian dolls and original christening gowns.

She resides in northern Virginia with her husband, taking much needed get-aways to their mountain home near the Blue Ridge Mountains, a place that evokes memories of days spent growing up in the Appalachian Mountains.

A lover of hats, she has worn many. Following marriage to her college sweetheart, and as wife, mother, grandmother, teacher, tutor, artist, writer, poet and crafter, she is a lover of art and antiques, surrounding herself, always, with books, seeking to learn more.

In 2015 she authored *Looking for Rainbows, Poetry, Prose and Art*, and in 2017, *Dark Side of the Moon*. Both books of mostly narrative poetry were published by Inner Child Press and were edited by hulya n. yilmaz.

in 2019, No Illusions.Through the Looking Glass, which was nominated to be considered for a Pulitzer Prize by the publisher and editor of InnerChild Press, ltd.

http://www.innerchildpress.com/jackie-davis-allen.php
jackiedavisallen.com

Jackie Davis Allen

A Blue Eyed, Blond Haired... Artist

Paul Higgins Stevenson, curiously, changed
His name to Pablo Estaban O'Higgins.
Born March 1904 in Salt Lake City, Utah.

Grew up in Utah and California, American-Mexican,
Studied at Academy of Arts in San Diego, won Soviet
Scholarship to the Academy of Art in Moscow.

Turned away from studying piano.
In 1924, became a student of Diego Rivera.
Himself, a painter muralist. And, a Communist.

For twenty years, 1927-1947,
Pablo O'Higgins, gifted with artistic talent,
Became a member of the Mexican Communist Party.

Died, July 1983, in Mexico City, Mexico.
Remembered by family, friends, Communists,
And leftist artists whose politics lean toward activism.

Shadows

She is entirely amenable
To learning something from him:
If he would but let her be herself.

She resents persistent attempts
To change her into a carbon copy of who,
Or what it is he thinks she should be or do.

Perhaps, a word of advice will suffice
To explain that she is happily content
With the person she is becoming.

And yet, with reflection, in time,
Might not mirror's illumination allow him
To see the light that's focused upon himself?

Self Talk

Heart thumping,
Breathing rapidly
Pressed down,
The walls are closing in.

Shame calls him a name.

Reverberating
Against window panes
The wind tangoes
With his fears and years.

Blame calls him a name.

In the darkness, he cowers
For he is but a shadow
Waiting, praying, for love
To call his name.

Tzemin Ition Tsai

Tzemin Ition Tsai

Dr. Tzemin Ition Tsai (蔡澤民博士) was born in Republic of China, in 1957. He holds a Ph.D. in Chemical Engineering and two Masters of Science in Applied Mathematics and Chemical Engineering. He is a professor at Asia University (Taiwan), editor of "Reading, Writing and Teaching" academic text. He also writes the long-term columns for Chinese Language Monthly in Taiwan.

He is a scholar with a wide range of expertise, while maintaining a common and positive interest in science, engineering and literature member. He is also an editor of "Reading, Writing and Teaching" academic text and a columnist for *'Chinese Language Monthly'* in Taiwan

He has won many national literary awards. His literary works have been anthologized and published in books, journals, and newspapers in more than 40 countries and have been translated into more than a dozen languages.

The Toiling Swallows Are Addicted To Dreams

Along the edge of the courtyard, the shadows of the sycamore trees follow the wind
The image of autumn trembles slightly at the tips of branch
On the top of the jade building, who is playing the jade flute?
Is it possible that besides me, there are still people who
ignore the low cloud covering the mountain in front of the building?
Seeing autumn so joyfully
Don't you see the August wind of last year?
The toiling swallows flew away, feeling melancholy at the loss of news with their family
My plates are full of simple diet but the willow trees standing in the water is so exuberant
I, a poor worker, can only use my arms as a pillow
Only the wearer knows where the shoe inches
However, the west wind only takes care of the sorrow of the guests
Rain has fallen
Pear blossoms fall all over the ground
Long night brings good dreams but it is still cold before dawn
Hometown dream, always
Never leave it to the swallows to end the morning conversation
Don't even learn the toiling swallows to addicted our dreams
I was squandering my half a hundred years, can it be that
Shouldn't sigh why I didn't miss my hometown when the dream is broken?

Horse Trail Mountain

Snow flies over the back of those ancient lamps
The geese lined up quietly passing by
Ah, That poor scholar
Could recognize the quilt that only covers the upper body
The small screen in front of the door
How long it has been standing by the side?
Looking at the horses on the slope far away calmly
Running wildly

The tears just wiped away
Poems written on the wall a long time ago
Hanging everywhere
Just like bunch after bunch of silk
Fine jade panpipe carried the sadness that can't be covered
Blowing leisurely night after night
Ah, My plum blossoms full of mountains
Do you know this?

That Roaming Figure Beyond The Great Wall

The scenery of Northland
Thousands of miles away, the ice field seals the dust
Thousands of miles away, the snow is floating everywhere
Looking through the inside and outside of the Great Wall,
only a vast white plain remains
Up and down of the big river, the turbulent water suddenly
stopped surging
The mountains brandish the silver python
Like a herd of elephants galloping under the full moon,
striving to be higher than the sky

The landscape in front is so gorgeous
Countless heroes have been conquered
What a pity
Both the first emperors of Qin and Han
Slightly but not suffused in literary talent
Taizong Emperors of the Tang and Song Dynasties
Couldn't par excellence in a unique style
The person specially favoured by heaven, Genghis Khan,
Only knows how to pull to bend the big bow, to shoot the
eagles
It's all over with time
Today
No one knows yet
Who are the truly great men of our time

Shareef Abdur Rasheed

Shareef Abdur Rasheed

Shareef Abdur-Rasheed, AKA Zakir Flo was born and raised in Brooklyn, New York. His education includes Brooklyn College, Suffolk County Community College and Makkah, Saudi Arabia. He is a Veteran of the Viet Nam era, where in 1969 he reverted to his now reverently embraced Islamic Faith. He is very active in the Islamic community and beyond with his teachings, activism and his humanity.

Shareef's spiritual expression comes through the persona of "Zakir Flo" . Zakir is Arabic for "To remind". Never silent, Shareef Abdur-Rasheed is always dropping science, love, consciousness and signs of the time in rhyme.

Shareef is the Patriarch of the Abdur-Rasheed Family with 9 Children (6 Sons and 3 Daughters) and 41 Grandchildren (24 Boys and 17 Girls).

For more information about Shareef, visit his personal FaceBook Page at :

https://www.facebook.com/shareef.abdurrasheed1
https://zakirflo.wordpress.com

O' Higgins

artist of the salt
capture humanity
salt of earth
Pablo exhibited
plight of mass's
work to survive
staying alive
everyday workers
told story of survival
message resonated
promote value of
working class families
diamond in the rough
pearl in oyster
not elitist bourgeoisie
living in fantasy
earth revolves around me
told the story of reality
his art of humanity

frontal lobotomy

vegetative state what's left of me
not the way Allah(swt) created me
opened my mouth and my brain
was taken to be studied in
some state sponsored lab latter
lab rats in a nation
where they use behavioral modification
if what you got to say resonates
with significant population
igniting thought raising conscious
make dem get up, stand up, speak up
for their rights
speaking truth to power
seeking justice must be intelligent
thought out
not just spewing words out the mouth
chanting empty slogans
then get arrested, beat
only for the same ol, same ol repeat
innocent children gunned down in
the street
they always wanted you to smile
even while the bodies pile
keeping the people docile
we'll just keep your brains awhile
you'll be good to go
as we maintain the status quo
reduced to data
like Hannibal Lecter serving your
brains up on a platter.
food4thought = education

Shareef Abdur Rasheed

Kimberly Burnham

Kimberly Burnham

A brain health expert with a PhD in Integrative Medicine, Kimberly Burnham has lived in tropical Colombia; in Belgium during the Vietnam War; in Japan teaching businessmen English; in diverse international Toronto, Canada; and several places in the US. Now, she's in Spokane, WA with her wife, Elizabeth, two sets of twins (age 11 & 14) and three dogs. Her recent book, *Awakenings: Peace Dictionary, Language and the Mind, a Daily Brain Health Program* includes the word for peace in hundreds of languages. Her poetry weaves through 80+ volumes of *The Year of the Poet, Inspired by Gandhi, Women Building the World*, and *A Woman's Place in the Dictionary*. She is currently working on several ekphrastic writing projects. One is a novel, *Art Thief Cracks Healing Code for Parkinson's Disease* and the other is non-fiction, *Using Ekphrastic Fiction Writing and Poetry to Create Interest and Promote Artists, Writers, and Poets*.

http://www.NerveWhisperer.Solutions

https://healthy-brain.medium.com/bears-at-the-window-of-climate-change-d1fb403eeaf3

Blue

Blue collars
shirt sleeves rolled up
ready to work
to serve
to see
decide
all in blue
colors of water and fear
and boys turning into men
the throat sending air and sound
pouring through a narrow place
creating words out of energy
expressing what is desperately desired
to fix
our community launches the best
we can be

At The Border

Fate of birth at the border

you there

on the other side

othered by me

here seeing you across

a bit of land

water where fish swim

back and forth

not knowing this is the border

blissfully ignorant birds fly

landing on this side then that

oblivious of the power that divides

the fates of you and I

Build a Free World

Free of hate
discrimination
and pain

Build a free world

Welcome, do something great
learn determination
experience joyful gain

Build a free world

Open the abundance gate
love creation
jump on the opportunity train

Build a free world
for everyone

Elizabeth E. Castillo

Elizabeth Esguerra Castillo

Elizabeth Esguerra Castillo is a multi-awarded and an Internationally-Published Contemporary Author/Poet and a Professional Writer / Creative Writer / Feature Writer / Journalist / Travel Writer from the Philippines. She has 2 published books, "Seasons of Emotions" (UK) and "Inner Reflections of the Muse", (USA). Elizabeth is also a co-author to more than 60 international anthologies in the USA, Canada, UK, Romania, India. She is a Contributing Editor of Inner Child Magazine, USA and an Advisory Board Member of Reflection Magazine, an international literary magazine. She is a member of the American Authors Association (AAA) and PEN International.

Web links:

Facebook Fan Page

https://free.facebook.com/ElizabethEsguerraCastillo

Google Plus

https://plus.google.com/u/0/+ElizabethCastillo

A Free World

People struggle to belong

In a world full of discrimination

The greatest dream of man

Is to live in a free world

Embracing the concept of oneness.

It's all beyond one's color, one's race

One's ethnicity, one's beliefs

To be free is to liberate

To let compassion and unity win

For in the end, love is the only cure.

I Am Woman

I am woman from the genes of Eve,
I may be a temptress at times
But the world can never be without me,
Cities have fallen down, enemies defeated
Because of great women seeking the truth.
Joan of Arc was one of them,
A woman warrior, a Blessed saint
Role model of a fierce woman
But never losing her femininity
Worthy to be idolized by many.
What is the essence of being a woman?
We learn calmness from her softness,
She is the light in the dark
A source of hope and inspiration,
Admired by the whole world.

The Bareness of Trees

Misty dew drops from the sky fall
Mixing with every tears I cried,
Does it hide the pain, the grief, the loss?
Somehow it masks the emptiness of the soul.
The autumn leaves left scars at dawn
When you chose to chase the light
The bareness of trees signifies your absence
When everywhere I look,
There's no trace of your shadow
And I ask myself, would I be fine?
Every piece of music we played lingers
Bringing tears to my eyes and once again
With every breath my mind drifts to thoughts of you.
Until the last leaf falls,
Revealing the nakedness of the trees
Below an overcast sky over a downpour
The bareness of trees, branches ran dry
Unlike the welling up of tears in my eyes,
An artist can paint the sorrowful aura
Where the trees have grown on a barren land
Alas, when the sun sets again over the horizon
Until the hues of the rainbow cheers me up once more
Behind the veil where angels ascend,
I await for spring to come to witness the blooms take over the gloom.

Joe Paire

Joe Paire

Joseph L Paire' aka Joe DaVerbal Minddancer . . .
is a quiet man, born in a time where civil liberties were a walk on thin ice. He's been a victim of his own shyness often sidelined in his own quest for love. He became the observer, charting life's path. Taking note of the why, people do what they do. His writings oft times strike a cord with the dormant strings of the reader. His pen the rosined bow drawn across the mind. He comes full-frontal or in the subtlest way, always expressing in a way that stimulate the senses.

www.facebook.com/joe.minddancer

Joe Paire

No More Divided

One table seven minds as we climb.
Words within the lines express our oneness.
Souls were lost although we all want this.
The struggle for just being is far reaching.
For whatever season through its teachings.
The common goal for all mankind is to be believed in.

Pick a race no; you can't.
Humanity doesn't exist without every man.
We eat we drink; we work we rest; we laugh we play.
Some don't and some pray, check your congregation.
At the end of the day, we all go through life's progressions.
Question: Do you know that person who's always late?

Do you know that person who can never wait?
Do you that person who just ate, and asking for yours?
Well, I'm asking you to explore the possibilities.
Of working together without mirror imagery
Philosophies know no boundaries.
It's based on the bias of humanity.

Who truly knows how our planet managed to be?
We managed the un-answerable to separate beliefs.
And all these things mean we are no more divided.
I gathered this from an image by Pablo O' Higgins.
From the point of his works there was nothing hidden
If justice is blind; how can we make the right decisions?

It's Okay

If it brings you to the point of contact, it's okay.
If you find yourself tracing steps, it's okay.
When tears fall over nothing at all.
When years stalled knowing you could have done better.
Now this weather, you don't know whether you should.
You know it's better that you could because you're okay.

I snapped a shot of a daffodil on my lot.
It was cold and nearly froze but it's yellow is hot.
If natures display comes out to express themselves
It's okay to enjoy the sunrise as you imagined.
This is what happens when you capture you.
The pure beauty of you comes out in a solum thought.

There are three now, the daffodils, the yellow ones.
They set in a scene of filled in well.
There was nothing left of the well whence it came.
It's okay to lay a lame rhyme from time to time.
I mindset of no regrets, know regret, it's okay.
We spend our whole lives trying to keep from dying.

It's okay not to say, it's okay if you do.
It's okay if you rock how you've always rocked you.
After all you've gotten through, claim your peace.
No flames in speech can reach your level of cool.
No one can teach your level of schooling.
And ruling! "Forget about it" I read about it.

It's okay, it's okay, it's okay, it's always been.

Joe Paire

Surrounded by Love

What keeps me from screaming and scheming,
Dreaming always helped to escape.
Call it fate or the gatekeeper is well aware of me.
I remember things erased by progression.
I remember things that I should have forgotten.
Forgiveness is rotten but vengeance is taught and.
I left love hanging still hanging in the hammock.

No 6 by 9 time to rewind.
Just my minds crimes to be found.
I need not be around myself.
I heed not the laws of social grace.
These are the flaws of time and space.

I'm surrounded by the cries of a toddler.
The tantrums' the screaming, the I can't believe things.
The way she just see's things, and dolls can talk.
She crawls and barks when she directs the scene.
Plastic inanimate objects
set like she was Spielberg's daughter.
She yells cut, then "Papa" "I hurt."
I don't know why she won't take off her boots.

They're cute, Frozen, like the way they stay on her feet.
She's dancing now, but I swear she can sing.
But I sink back into disparity, clarity is brown.
Love is clear, without cheers and I'm surrounded
I rarely speak on profoundness but thank you.

hülya n. yılmaz

hülya n. yılmaz

Professor Emerita (Humanities, Penn State, USA), hülya n. yılmaz [sic] is a published tri-lingual author, literary translator, and Director of Editing Services (Inner Child Press International, USA). Her work has appeared in numerous anthologies of global endeavors and was presented at poetry events in the U.S. and abroad. In 2018, the WIN of British Colombia, Canada honored yılmaz with a literary excellence award. Her two poems remain permanently installed in *Telepoem Booth* (USA). hülya finds it vital for everyone to understand a deeper sense of self, and writes creatively to attain a comprehensive awareness for and development of our humanity.

Writing Web Site
https://hulyanyilmaz.com/

Editing Web Site
https://hulyasfreelancing.com

The Meeting

a painting by Pablo O'Higgins
catches the eye
it is said to be
representing unity within humanity
the banner on this artwork claims thus:
"Build a free world. No masters. No slaves."
Signed: "Makers of the world united"

a portrayal of men only . . .
Caucasians only . . .
clothing . . . differentiated by class
mimics and gestures of the few front-view men
stress who has the last word

unity within humanity?
"Makers of the world united"?
i, for one, do not think so!

this visual art is more like an emphasis on hierarchy
amidst various segments of societal authority . . .

skin hues

what i am about to say is a no-brainer, for sure
my intent is not to assault your intellect
but rather to express the most obvious
so that none of us attempts to disrespect
the basic reality of our humanity
any longer

we are all born with melanin in our bodies
some of us have more of this natural pigment
while children are blind to such nuances
(unless they are taught at home)
as adults, some of us beg to differ
we then choose to go against the stream,
disrupting the most natural flow:
all for one, one for all
for the sake of harmony within humanity

skin hues, thus, become a means to hate,
to hate unconditionally and passionately
it is only a matter of a short time then
before that hatred turns into sizable inheritances
for generations to come

on account of our outer traits . . .

on account of variations in our pigments . . .

what a badge of shame
to wear as the heritage of one's family!

hülya n. yılmaz

struggles

art to signify

labor and revolution

true dedication

Teresa E. Gallion

Teresa E. Gallion

Teresa E. Gallion was born in Shreveport, Louisiana and moved to Illinois at the age of 15. She completed her undergraduate training at the University of Illinois Chicago and received her master's degree in Psychology from Bowling Green State University in Ohio. She retired from New Mexico state government in 2012.

She moved to New Mexico in 1987. While writing sporadically for many years, in 1998 she started reading her work in the local Albuquerque poetry community. She has been a featured reader at local coffee houses, bookstores, art galleries, museums, libraries, Outpost Performance Space, the Route 66 Festival in 2001 and the State of Oklahoma's Poetry Festival in Cheyenne, Oklahoma in 2004. She occasionally hosts an open mic.

Teresa's work is published in numerous Journals and anthologies. She has two CDs: *On the Wings of the Wind* and *Poems from Chasing Light*. She has published three books: *Walking Sacred Ground, Contemplation in the High Desert* and *Chasing Light*.

Chasing Light was a finalist in the 2013 New Mexico/Arizona Book Awards.

The surreal high desert landscape and her personal spiritual journey influence the writing of this Albuquerque poet. When she is not writing, she is committed to hiking the enchanted landscapes of New Mexico. You may preview her work at

http://bit.ly/1aIVPNq or *http://bit.ly/13IMLGh*

Marking Territory

They gather at the table
with stern faces
ready for the verbal fight.

Whose voice will be the loudest?
Who will control the fiery
blood before the physical battle?

The burning glare in each eye
holds the tales of each warrior clan.
Each male releases his inner power
to the table.

Scratching every word in the paper
with his mark
like raising his leg to mark territory.

Who will be king of the table today?

Miracle in the Woods

There is a miracle in the woods
with her name on it
running through the trees.

Gratitude floods her eyelids.
The light streams bend her knees
in reverence for the woods.

She looks beyond the breeze
caught in deep space thoughts.
Eyes burn with intensity.

Her soul floats in front of her
boldly moving as if
a musical sonata plays just for her.

Look for Your Name

I can see the laughter
behind your teardrops
trying to expose your joy.

You fight so hard
to mask your feelings
in the fields of pain.

Fear is a stifling bull
whose horns must be cut
so you can rise with the sun.

Love is coming
on a black stallion
to rescue your soul.

Keep watching the horizon.
Sunrise expands each day.
Your name floats in the light.

Ashok K. Bhargava

Ashok K. Bhargava

Ashok Bhargava is a poet, writer, community activist, public speaker, management consultant and a keen photographer. Based in Vancouver, he has published several collections of his poems: Riding the Tide, Mirror of Dreams, A Kernel of Truth, Skipping Stones, Half Open Door and Lost in the Morning Calm. His poetry has been published in various literary magazines and anthologies.

Ashok is a Poet Laureate and poet ambassador to Japan, Korea and India. He is founder of WIN: Writers International Network Canada. Its main objective is to inspire, encourage, promote and recognize writers of diverse genres, artists and community leaders. He has received many accolades including Nehru Humanitarian Award for his leadership of Writers International Network Canada, Poets without Borders Peace Award for his journeys across the globe to celebrate peace and to create alliances with poets, and Kalidasa Award for creative writings.

Pretense of a Promise

each dream lingers
each bud soaked in tears
nourishes the bloom

day after day
breathing in the air
that destroys the body

the smell of neglect
is the only thing
that is assured

rebellious minds skitter
unanswered prayers
ambiguous future

rhymes of life
bruise
with fake sacraments

the night
pushes away the light
of the setting sun

nothing lasts
of promise
such is the promise of light

bare hands
toil hard
beg for mercy

silently
tolerating excesses
that's all they can do

Sweet Surrender

you and me
flow into each other
as wave into a wave

we drift towards ocean
without knowing the way

we need not to know
the flowing to flow
to immerse

we connect
a raindrop
a teardrop

unconsciously flow
to something sacred
and cease to exist

Empty Nest

a scribbled image
reveals the impression

you left for me to keep.

childhood behind
you moved on

on your own.

memories like
baseball cards

still in the dressers.

your jersey holds me tight
the way your tiny arms

wrapped me.

*This poem is about my son leaving home.

Caroline 'Ceri Naz' Nazareno Gabis

Carolin 'Ceri' Nazareno-Gabis

Caroline 'Ceri Naz' Nazareno-Gabis, author of Velvet Passions of Calibrated Quarks, World Poetry Canada International Director to Philippines is known as a 'poet of peace and friendship', a multi-awarded poet, editor, journalist, speaker, linguist, educator, peace and women's advocate. She believes that learning other's language and culture is a doorway to wisdom.

Among her poetic belts include PANORAMA YOUTH LITERARY AWARDS 2020, 7 th Prize Winner in the 19th, 20th and 21st Italian Award of Literary Festival; Writers International Network-Canada "Amazing Poet 2015", The Frang Bardhi Literary Prize 2014 (Albania), the sair-gazeteci or Poet Journalist Award 2014 (Tuzla, Istanbul, Turkey) and World Poetry Empowered Poet 2013 (Vancouver, Canada). She's a featured member of Association of Women's Rights and Development (AWID), The Poetry Posse, Galaktika Poetike, Asia Pacific Writers and Translators (APWT), Axlepino and Anacbanua.

Her poetry and children's stories have been featured in different anthologies and magazines worldwide.

Links to her works:

panitikan.ph/2018/03/30/caroline-nazareno-gabis

apwriters.org/author/ceri_naz/

www.aveviajera.org/nacionesunidasdelasletras/id1181.html

The Muralist

He put revolts in the streets,
Words scattered like nymphs
Whimsical parabolic hues
Take revenge on the wooden fences,
At night, the village has faceless shadows
There are squalling babies
Close to the clinic rooms,
Then he filled his cup
With great eagerness
To finish the meandered
Land, air, water themes.

His rolling paintbrush
Were like playing a solitaire
Deck of spades, flowers, hearts and more
Then the queen, just passed him by,
He sniffed the bubble gum scent,
And was mesmerized
To mix more colors in his bucket.

A young boy kissing his mother's cheeks
He grabbed his eyeglasses, pressing the wall
Butterflies, birds, flowers, and bees
And a couple wearing tropical shirts,
His arms console century trees,
Whistled and hummed ''Fly me to the moon''
His masterpiece smiles
Thousand times and more.

Formulas on Fire

Remember the formulas you learned from
An Organic Chemistry class,
You have soaked from grins
But calmed by marmalade and *pan de sal*,
And *kopiko* on the side to
Wake you up,
So you will solve the alluring empirical
Mutations in your brain,
Causing a domino effect
To your carpals and lumbar parts.

And if it's time to sleep,
There are parading pre-nightmares
into your pillows,
Re-calculating again
And again.
You got it almost perfect,
Then you got up again,
Reviewing the last unit,
Suddenly, the Lee Min Ho portrait
Collapsed your membranes
To giggles,
Brought you another norturnal agenda
You want another Korean novella,

The google classroom has a reminder,
You have at least few seconds to send
Your chemistry revolution assignment.
Time is up!

Carolin 'Ceri' Nazareno-Gabis

Her Majesty
For All the Women Heroes

She creates like Isis;

she owns the sky, the sun and the moon.

the alchemic maxim of force and femininity;

She rules like Hathor;

she wears the crown of love, joy, music, dance,

 motherhood and fertility;

She wins like Artemis; she is fearless, strong,

 adventurous, and youthful.

She is March.

 The birthmark of empowered homeless suns.

Swapna Behera

Swapna Behera

Swapna Behera is a bilingual contemporary poet, author, translator and editor from Odisha, India. She was a teacher from 1984 to 2015. Her stories, poems and articles are widely published in National and International journals, and ezines, and are translated into different national and International languages. She has penned six books. She is the recipient of the Prestigious International Mother Language UGADI AWARD WINNER 2019. She was conferred upon the Prestigious International Poesis Award of Honor at the 2nd Bharat Award for Literature as Jury in 2015, The Enchanting Muse Award in India World Poetree Festival 2017, World Icon of Peace Award in 2017, and the Pentasi B World Fellow Poet in 2017. She is the recipient of the Prolific Poetess Award ,The Life time Achievement Award ,The Best Planner Award ,The Sahitya Shiromani Award, ATAL BIHARI BAJPAYEE Award, ATAL Award 2018 ,Global Literature Guardian Award ,International Life Time Achievement Award and the Master of Creative Impulse Award .She has received the Honoured Poet of India from the Seychelles Government accredited Literary Society Lasher one poem A NIGHT IN THE REFUGEE CAMP is translated into 60 languages .She is the Ambassador of Humanity by Hafrikan Prince Art World Africa 2018 and an official member of World Nation's Writers Union ,Kazakhstan2018. Italy, the National President for India by Hispanomundial Union of Writers (UHE), Peru, the administrator of several poetic groups, and the Cultural Ambassador for India and South Asia of Inner Child Press African is the life member of Odisha Environmental Society.

swapna.behera@gmail.com

Building A Free World

building a free world
is as simple as boiling rice on the fire
making foams in the tea cup
taking a decision for each
reaching every heart
where there are no masters
no slaves
a clarion call to the workers of the world to unite
only to remember those syllables
holding hands
unscrolling the message
migrants, labours
synonyms of hammer and sickles
grow and le others grow
simple journey is so difficult
for there are parasites
who live on the sweating, bloods of others?
can the tear ever replace the?
with all strength to fight against discrimination
a muralist of post revolution movement
the journey id
towards

Catch Me If You Can

I am on my way to the
roots of my homeland
where the jasmines
are spread
on the road
hunger is deciphered to smiles
no metallic metaphors
no zigzag jingles
no demon; no goddess
only me and my being
seed, soil and song
no death no birth
no cursor, no internet
no tickets, no money
no numbers, no hidden agenda
no formal dress, no horse race
no breaking, no anguish
no lust, no back counting
only fresh alphabets
I am walking with slow pace
catch me if you can
I am beyond your reach
certainly, I am beyond ...

Shame on You

shame on you
dear brothers and sisters
you are always missing
missing in summer and in winter
when someone needs you
needs your response
needs you to listen

how do you expect?
the trees never react
they can never sit
in your air-conditioned seminars
or zoom meets
to discuss their post operation plights
your electric axe is so sharp
you have cut their tongues, lips, hands and feet
shame on you!

you earn curse of the leaves and flowers
the squirrels are gazing at you
with innocent eyes

shame on you
for you can disturb every one
the bees, birds, butterflies, birds
and whole bunch of their clan
who has authorised you?
in primal sadness

how tenderly the buds pray
where are you from?
where is

your city?
your muscle power is so terminal
shame on you
the tree still smiles and fills your lungs ....

Swapna Behera

Albert 'Infinite' Carrasco

Albert 'Infinite' Carassco

Albert "Infinite The Poet" Carrasco is an urban poet, mentor and public speaker.

Albert believes his experience of growing up in poverty, dealing with drugs and witnessing murder over and over were lessons learnt, in order to gain knowledge to teach. Albert's harsh reality and honesty is a powerfully packed punch delivered through rhyme. Infinite grew up in the east part of the Bronx and still resides there, so he knows many young men will follow the same dark path he followed looking for change. The life of crime should never be an option to being poor but it is, very often.

Infinite poetry @lulu.com

Alcarrasco2 on YouTube

Infinite the poet on reverbnation

Infinite Poetry

http://www.lulu.com/us/en/shop/al-infinite-carrasco/infinite-poetry/paperback/product-21040240.html

Pablo O'Higgins

A moment in time, during a meeting of minds.
I see an artist depiction of wanting out poverty and oppression.
I see a blueprint of revolution.
Hands are shaking as ideas for a better life are in the making.
It almost looks like "The Last Supper",
Instead of apostles there's ordinary people with hopes and dreams
to live in a world in the near future,
where families wouldn't have to live, to suffer.
There's a band of brothers uplifting each other,
A bunch of diamonds in the rough wanting the world to shine brighter.
All they want to see is unity and equality.
Pablo shows it with his concrete image artistry.

Failed to Succeed

I lived a harsh life and learned harsh lessons in these New York slums. Fails helped me succeed, I've been educated through experiences most wouldn't want to experience, so I share bars of scars by making my pen bleed. Everyday I wake up is a blessing, I thank the almighty for his guidance, had to witness joy and pain, sunshine and rain, so I laughed, cried, smiled and frowned dealing with the ghetto pestilence in order to overstand and teach the pros and cons of red money violence. I swear when I reflect it feels as if those reflections were a dream, they're nightmarish reactions to past actions, unfortunately they're nonfiction. A lot of men didn't get to celebrate being twenty one because at sixteen, seventeen, eighteen, nineteen and twenty they were victims of redrum. I grew up with good friends. I was the youngest, I did what they did, they did what I did, we walked the same paths as kids. When I was younger I wondered why they're in heaven and why was I left to deal with poverty's oppression?, as I got older and wiser I realized God saved me to rewind time with my mind after living out their forever, to dissect history with literature that will educate the future.

The voices are quarreling

Do that, do this. No don't do it. I brought you this far, I need to go further faster. One voice wants me to prosper, the other says the same but ends with some sinister laughter. Take cautious steps, let's ride to the death. The next step is coming, make it happen now, why wait? It's a mental Armageddon that leads to an unwanted fate.

Weigh your options, the scale is even. Do good, do bad too be good. Your almost out, go back to the hood. reach your goal, do what you know. That's a righteous conscious and the temptations of evil conversing in ones cerebral. Follow me, commit blaspheme.

Hydroplane to the top, float on phlebotomy. That's the voices inside of me.. That's a person trying to deal with todays economy.

Eliza Segiet

Eliza Segiet

Eliza Segiet: Master's Degree in Philosophy, completed postgraduate studies in Cultural Knowledge, Philosophy, Arts and Literature at Jagiellonian University. She is a member of The Association of Polish Writers and The NWNU - Union of Writers of the World.

Her poems *Questions* and *Sea of Mists* won the title of the International Publication of the Year 2017 and 2018 in Spillwords Press.

For her volume of *Magnetic People* she won a literary award of a *Golden Rose* named after Jaroslaw Zielinski (Poland 2019 r.). Her poem The *Sea of Mists* was chosen as one of the best one hundred poems of 2018 by International Poetry Press Publication Canada.
In Poet's Yearbook, as the author of *Sea of Mists*, she was awarded with the prestigious Elite Writer's Status Award as one of the best poets of 2019 (July 2019).
She was awarded *World Poetic Star Award* by World Nations Writers Union – the world's largest Writers' Union from Kazakhstan (August 2019).
In September 2019 she was 1st Place Laureate (Foreign Poetry category) – in Contest *Quando È la Vita ad Invitare* for poem *Be Yourself* (Italy).
Her poem *Order* from volume *Unpaired* was selected as one of the 100 best poems of 2019 in International Poetry Press Publications (Canada).
Nominated for the Pushcart Prize 2019.
Nominated for the iWoman Global Awards (2019).
Laureate Naji Naaman Literary Prize 2020.
Laureate International Award PARAGON OF HOPE (Canada, 2020).
Obtained certificate of appreciation from *Gujarat Sahitya Academy* and *Motivational Strips* for literary excellence par with global standards (2020).
Ambassador of Literature granted by *Motivational Strips*.
Author's works can be found in anthologies, separate books and literary magazines worldwide.

Without division
In memory of Pablo O'Higgins

On a way to freedom
there's no place for evil.
It's unavailing.
Target can be reached
by bluffing,
that we don't notice enemies.
Seeing but not responding,
intent comes to fruition.

Harmony
needs understanding,
but all
have laws and duties
 – Freedom for the world
 – Regard
with no segregation - for everyone.

Translated Ula de B.

Glow of the Eyes

Curious about the world,
with a chilled drink in hand
they admire the black land,
and the sight of the creviced earth
completes their needs.

At the same time
emaciated,
covered with flies,
children are fighting for life.

And they are there.
In the midst of ubiquitous poverty,
they see the magic of light,
and only later the glow of the eyes
of beautiful African women.

They are in the same place for years,
the same needs and a constant lack of water.
– So little
and not so little
to be able to live.

Translated by Artur Komoter

Barrage

She escaped from a place,
where the urban bustle
ceased to tempt her,
where the lit streets
no longer agitated.

Neon barrage of ads
of unnecessary,
bargain items
no longer lured.

It was so hard
to live in the hustle and bustle.

She loves silence –
now it is
her only friend.

Maybe something more,
but she doesn't give away.
for they will come thirsting
for paradise
to unwittingly break
the nest of peace.

Translated by Artur Komoter

William S. Peters Sr.

William S. Peters, Sr.

Bill's writing career spans a period of over 50 years. Being first Published in 1972, Bill has since went on to Author in excess of 50 additional Volumes of Poetry, Short Stories, etc., expressing his thoughts on matters of the Heart, Spirit, Consciousness and Humanity. His primary focus is that of Love, Peace and Understanding!

Bill says . . .

I have always likened Life to that of a Garden. So, for me, Life is simply about the Seeds we Sow and Nourish. All things we "Think and Do", will "Be" Cause and eventually manifest itself to being an "Effect" within our own personal "Existences" and "Experiences" . . . whether it be Fruit, Flowers, Weeds or Barren Landscapes! Bill highly regards the Fruits of his Labor and wishes that everyone would thus go on to plant "Lovely" Seeds on "Good Ground" in their own Gardens of Life!

to connect with Bill, he is all things Inner Child

www.iaminnerchild.com

Personal Web Site

www.iamjustbill.com

Pablo Esteban O'Higgins

Or was it . . .
Paul Higgins Stevenson,
Who am i?

Diego allowed me to work with him
And the influence of
My Mormonism ways
Did not get
In the way

Art was the movement
I embraced
And my Communistic ways
Was the path I travelled

Freedom to express my self
Without
Repressing
My self

Embracing my
Multi-culturalism
Rejecting the
Social isms
For I was a prism
Of creation

Pablo Esteban O'Higgins

Or was it . . .
Paul Higgins Stevenson,
Who am i?

Guess !

Question everything

Yeah,
Question everything!!!!
….
What are/is
The motive? ...
Behavioral modification?,
Mental colonization?

Where is the exit
From the box
We ALL are trapped in?

Where is the map
That will lead us
To that 'Promised Land'
Where men and women
And children
From all persuasions
Can stand
Hand in hand
With an acceptable peaceful understanding
That does not demand
Anyone to exercise
Their lower selves

Many, if not most
Have bought into the
'Columbus discovered America'
Syndrome ... or
Jesus had blonde hair,
White skin and
Blue eyes theorem ...

But, did you know
That lies told often enough
Become some folk's truth,
Even though their nature
Is still a 'Lie' ?

My oh my . . .

Toxicity for free
Is fed to us
Via the media,
Social platforms,
Billboards
And commercials ...
Which is everywhere
One looks,
Even in the books
One studies,
To supposedly ....
'Learn'

We must learn to discern,
Or we will burn
Down Hope's hope to acquire
All that humanity yearns ...
For

I went to the store
The other day,
Shopping for a miracle ...
....
I wanted to purchase
Something,
Anything,

Everything
That would sate this hunger,
Quench this thirst
That never leaves me

I did manage to quiet
The rumblings,
The yearnings,
But for a little while,
And wouldn't you know it,
Here I am ... back
Once again
In the store,
Looking for more
Treats and Tricks
Seeking to cessate
My insatiable need
To ...
Question everything

Question everything . . . even the questions !

Conundrum

We strive for it,
Knowing that the road
To its home
Will look unachievable,
But we must believe,
Don't we?

Utopia

Love of the purest essence
Evades our understanding,
Though we delude ourselves
In the telling of the incessant lies of
'I Love You'

Truth her self
Plays such games
With our small perspectives,
As she dances and hides
In the shadows of obscurity
Laughing to herself
About our silly vanities ...
But we seek her out
Just the same,
Never know
What she looks like,
Nor how she is dressed,
So we lean to our own
Feeble imaginings

Compassion,
True compassion,
What is it,
And where can it be found?

Though we tell ourselves,
That our hearts are contrite,
They are but empty vessels
Whose walls are filled
With mirrors of illusion,
For when has any one of us
Totally submitted
To anything?

Understanding ...
Is tethered loosely,
But securely
To a variable base of knowledge
That we think we possess,
But what is it we truly know of
That can stand the tests
Of time?

I tried to listen,
But there was noise

I attempted to quiet my thoughts,
But my thoughts were
Of the quiet I created

I knew not how to yield
When it was required,
And still
After the many years

William S. Peters, Sr.

Of alacrity,
I still am that spun bundle of energy
Seeking a place
To definitively unwind
And cut the bonds
That define me,
But then,
Whose task would that be
To explain to 'Self', my self
Where the path begins
To 'nowhere'

Everywhere I look,
I am blinded
By the activities of mind-stuff,
A consciousness that abides,
So where belies the resolution
To these spoken conundrums?

It is said "seek and you shall find" ...
I say ...
"don't seek, and 'it' shall find you!!!"

April 2021 Featured Poets

~ * ~

Katarzyna Brus- Sawczuk

Anwesha Paul

Rozalia Aleksandrova

Shahid Abbas

Katarzyna Brus-Sawczuk

Katarzyna Brus-Sawczuk

The author is a doctor of Medical Sciences, specialist in microscopy endodontics, teacher in Warsaw Medical University. She writes poems and short prosaic forms. She is a member of the Associacion of Polish Authors (SAP.) Her poems have been published in a lot of polish antologies and were recognized in poetry competitions. She has published 3 poetic volumes. Poems and prose touch the choices, emotions, they carry a certain loneliness, do not give unambiguous answers. Closed rows are the key word that turns out to be a surprising title. Such a construction has become a characteristic sign of the poet.

Katarzyna Brus-Sawczuk

The Moment of Beginning

Dessert wind
brings the shadow
of ancient trees
the wind whispers
wisely
in heads of old people
shisha smoke
wraps the air
in river line
between two borders
first babtism
connects people
separates nations
the wind blows
afterall gently freezes

Women Power

Burj …
lights
possesion of the brain
American girls, European
women from Lebannon
Emirates
intersection of cultures
muslim mullah
singing a prayer
city noise
languages mixture
beautiful girls
dancing
in high hills
eyes without faces
in black
intoxicating scent
of perfume
women like flowers
distant memory
freedom how do we
understand?

Fish- Sign of Life

Today I have sent sms
to God online
instead of a postcard
with a wishful thinking
virually
I won't wait
for a personal answer
about an unlimited hate
about a stupitidy
about a state of my soul
about a tricky
plan
of our enemies
-praying
I cuddle to the cold wall
warmed up with
a touch of humans'
presence
four- armed cross
I weigh in my hand
trying to understand
the lack of conscience

Anwesha Paul

Anwesha Paul

Anwesha Paul is an animation film-maker and user experience design specialist working as a Manager with PwC to create original visual content. She has ten years of experience in visual design, storytelling and scripting for the screen. She is also a writer and speaker having contributed pieces to 'The Statesman' since her childhood and conducting design workshops in Rwanda, Kathmandu and La Martiniere for Girls' School, Kolkata in addition to her own workplace PwC. She is an award-winning animation film maker with screenings in several film festivals across the world. She has designed book covers for Routledge and Orient Blackswan, and has illustrated and designed for UNICEF, Rwanda and Room to Read.

Death and deathlessness

The wordless poem
The formless painting
The soundless song
The bottomless pit
The emptiness which defies definition
The crucible of dissolution

Ah! The freedom of being ness
The awareness of nothingness
Watching the waves of creation crash into the shores of non-existence
If this is death, then let me die to every moment
For I AM.

Wanderings

In the labyrinth of my mind
I walk through the scourge of time
In the hope to find
A little piece of paradise.

And when the piece cannot be found
I mine others' hearts for gold
And when I see their blackened soul
I recoil in horror recognising it to be my own.

Darkness

I exist.
Not visible to the eye
Subtler than air
In total silence
And in a deafening stillness
I exist.

I existed before time
And I will exist after it
For I am beyond it.

I exist.
Before the universe came into creation
For all arises from the womb of the void

And yet we fear
This nothingness.
This nothingness which is our mother and our grave.

Rozalia Aleksandrova

Rozalia Aleksandrova

Rozalia Aleksandrova lives in Plovdiv, Bulgaria. Author of 11 poetry books: "The House of My Soul" (2000), "Shining Body" (2003), "The Mystery of the Road" (2005), "The Eyes of the Wind" (2007) , "Parable of the key" (2008), "The Conversation between Pigeons" (2010), "Sacral" (2013), "The Real Life of Feelings" (2015), "Pomegranate from Narrow" (2016)… "Everything I did not say"(2019). Editor and compiler of over ten literary almanacs, collections and anthologies. He is a member of the Union of Bulgarian Writers. In 2006 he created a poetic-intellectual association "Quantum and Friends" for the promotion of quantum poetry in civil society, Plovdiv and Bulgarian phenomenon. Initiator and organizer of the International Festival of Poetry "SPIRITUALITY WITHOUT BORDERS".

Rozalia Aleksandrova

When Thoughts Draw A Road

When thoughts

draw a road

and shadows pierce the darkness.

A star burns

without flesh.

From the glowing ashes of our fire.

Followed by a meteor shower.

A sunny foal-like sparkle in the eye.

In amazing pure rye

a spark has flickered.

But thoughts draw a road.

And shadows sway.

Love is on its way.

And autumn goes insane.

Promegranate From An Alien

No matter if you love.

Or if you don't.

You are a cry

in the womb

of the Pomegranate.

Splattering

The Time

and Meaning

of the magical grains

for the nectar.

Rozalia Aleksandrova

***

My heart
is a verse,
which is writing
an ode
to you.

Shahid Abbas

Shahid Abbas

Shahid Abbas is a poet and writer, he was born in a village 421GB, Tandlianwala Faisalabad Pakistan. He studied first at the government degree college in Tandlianwala and also at GC University Faisalabad from where he attained a MA degree in English literature. He has worked as a teacher. Shahid began writing poetry when he was nineteen-years-old. He has received many writing awards from on line writing organisations. Shahid's poetry has been published in many international books also his stories in an international newspaper. At the present time, he is working on completing his own book.

Dear Almighty

We humbly beg your blessing
Forgetting to ask
We are helpless
Only you can save us

Throughout an ungrateful universe
People are dying
Souls savaged
The world has closed upon us
Lives ruined.....

Dear God protect us
Listen to the voices of the innocent still in
lockdown
Fear fear everywhere
Humans refusing to be human
Death wanders like shadow

You are the real King
Omnipresent
You alone can do for us
What we mortals only dream of
We are here to serve you
To do as you ask
We believe in You
Please forgive us

Darkness pervades
You are the pure light
Please show us the way
Almighty forgive us

We have forgotten your love
Roads are riddled with bodies
The graveyards filled

Dear God have mercy on us
We have forgotten
Only you can do the impossible
No matter we have worldly goods
We remain helpless and powerless
The heartless owners of universe spewing their empty lies
They do what they want
We are nothing to them
To you we are everything
Please save us
Only you can.....

Lessons from the Night

I turn to the night
Searching for some escape
to teach me lesson in love
and restore my lost heart and faith

Reminding me that I'm not perfect
The night and moon pass into one another
it's when she slips on her starry dress
That I see why she and the moon are perfect lovers

The moon adores her beauty
He shines his brightest pose for her
Awed by this beautiful duo
I sat down and watched in silent wonder

Too quickly Night turned from me
Refusing to stay much longer
No matter how much I plead with her
She says it's time to surrender

So many lovers has she
I declare love with them in unision
All the worlds moths and fireflies
Desire to drown in her flame in fusion

Morning appears as she prepares to vanish
Holding on is now futile
Rays of sun surround and warm me
Still I yearn for Night for more of a while

The sun scorns my desire and
the moon starts to fade away
Nay! says the sun to me
To see her, wait another day.

Love's Purity

When every word is love
How is it possible
The tongue speaks deceit

When the chest heaves
From a heavy heart
Can you speak of love's purity

Redeem me
in my suffering
Vindicate me
in an unspoken covenant
Forgive my iniquity
aspiring to fly to angels
I plummet in free fall to earth
with the mighty heft of stone

Point to the new reality
Turn to me in gratitude
I am lonely
Afflicted
Remorse imprisons
Release me from anguish
Look kindly upon my distress
Set my heart at rest

Let me not drop into the pit
Where lies deep shame
In you is my refuge
You protect me
In your promise is my hope

Shahid Abbas

Redeem me
A lost man stumbling
Mumbling words of despair
I surrender my anguish to you
Ecstasy and joy my sole rewards
My trouble sacrificed at your feet

Dance me to the moon
And please never ask why.....

Remembering

our fallen soldiers of verse

Janet Perkins Caldwell
February 14, 1959 ~ September 20, 2016

Alan W. Jankowski
16 March 1961 ~ 10 March 2017

Now available

World Healing World Peace
2020

Poets for Humanity

Inner Child Press News

Poetry Posse Members

We are so excited to share and announce a few of the current books, as well as the new and upcoming books of some of our Poetry Posse authors.

On the following pages we present to you ...

Jackie Davis Allen

Gail Weston Shazor

hülya n. yılmaz

Nizar Sartawi

Faleeha Hassan

Fahredin Shehu

Caroline 'Ceri' Nazareno

Eliza Segiet

Teresa E. Gallion

William S. Peters, Sr.

The Year of the Poet VIII ~ April 2021

Now Available
www.innerchildpress.com

Inner Child Press News

Now Available
www.innerchildpress.com

Now Available at

www.amazon.com/gp/product/B08MYL5B7S/ref=dbs_a_def_rwt_hsch_vapi_tkin_p1_i2

Inner Child Press News

Now Available at
www.innerchildpress.com

The Year of the Poet VIII ~ April 2021

Now Available
www.innerchildpress.com

Inner Child Press News

Now Available
www.innerchildpress.com

The Year of the Poet VIII ~ April 2021

Now Available
www.innerchildpress.com

Inner Child Press News

COMING SOON
www.innerchildpress.com

The Year of the Poet VIII ~ April 2021

Now Available
www.innerchildpress.com

The Book of krisar

Volume I

william s. peters, sr.

The Book of krisar

Volume II

william s. peters, sr.

Inner Child Press News

Now Available
www.innerchildpress.com

The Book of krisar

Volume III

william s. peters, sr.

The Book of krisar

Volume IV

william s. peters, sr.

The Year of the Poet VIII ~ April 2021

Now Available
www.innerchildpress.com

Inner Child Press News

Now Available
www.innerchildpress.com

The Year of the Poet VIII ~ April 2021

Private Issue
www.innerchildpress.com

Inner Child Press News

Now Available
www.innerchildpress.com

The Year of the Poet VIII ~ April 2021

Now Available at
www.innerchildpress.com

Inner Child Press News

Now Available at
www.innerchildpress.com

The Year of the Poet VIII ~ April 2021

Now Available at
www.innerchildpress.com

Inner Child Press News

Now Available at
www.innerchildpress.com

HERENOW

FAHREDIN SHEHU

The Year of the Poet VIII ~ April 2021

Now Available at
www.innerchildpress.com

Inner Child Press News

Now Available at
www.innerchildpress.com

The Year of the Poet VIII ~ April 2021

Now Available at
www.innerchildpress.com

Inner Child Press News

Now Available at
www.innerchildpress.com

The Year of the Poet VIII ~ April 2021

Now Available at
www.innerchildpress.com

Inner Child Press News

Now Available at
www.innerchildpress.com

Breakfast

for

Butterflies

Faleeha Hassan

The Year of the Poet VIII ~ April 2021

Now Available at
www.innerchildpress.com

7 Days in Palestine

william s. peters sr.

Inner Child Press News

Now Available at
www.innerchildpress.com

The Year of the Poet VIII ~ April 2021

Now Available at
www.innerchildpress.com

Inner Child Press News

Now Available at
www.innerchildpress.com

Think on These Things
Book II

william s. peters, sr.

Other Anthological works from

Inner Child Press International

www.innerchildpress.com

Inner Child Press Anthologies

World Healing World Peace 2020

Poets for Humanity

Now Available

www.worldhealingworldpeacepoetry.com

Inner Child Press Anthologies

Now Available
www.innerchildpress.com

Inner Child Press Anthologies

Inner Child Press International
&
The Year of the Poet
present

Poetry
the best of 2020

Poets of the World

Now Available
www.innerchildpress.com

Inner Child Press Anthologies

Now Available
www.innerchildpress.com

Inner Child Press Anthologies

words for a better tomorrow

The Conscious Poets

Now Available
www.innerchildpress.com

Inner Child Press Anthologies

Now Available
www.innerchildpress.com

Inner Child Press Anthologies

Now Available at
www.innerchildpress.com

Inner Child Press Anthologies

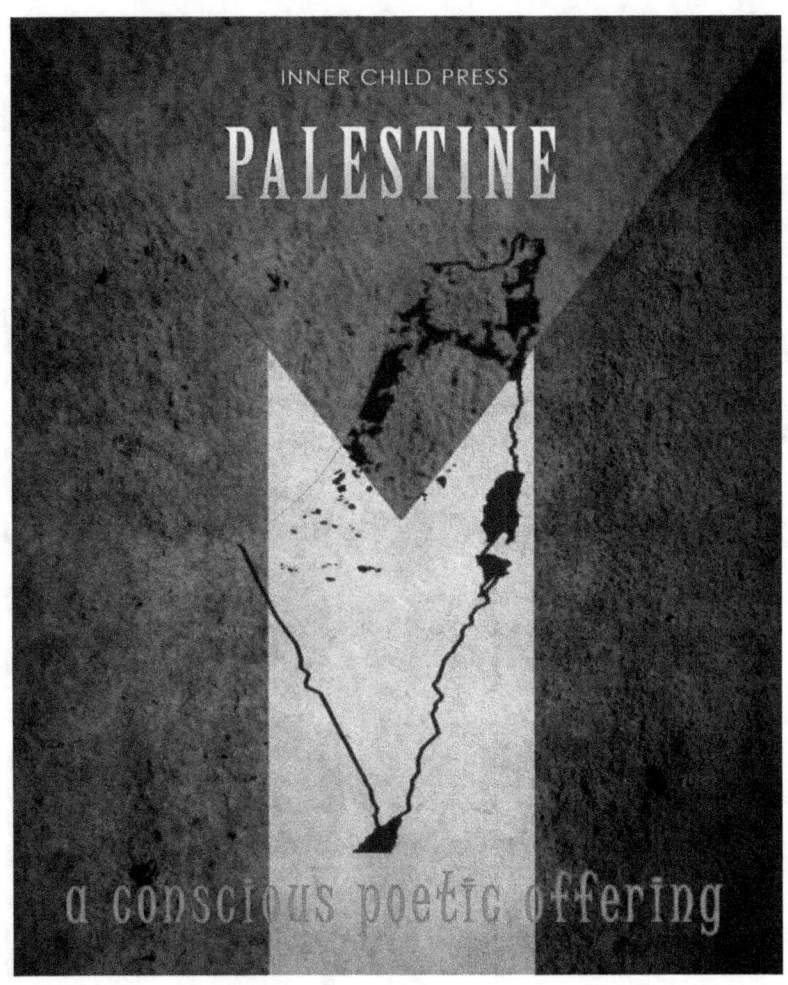

Now Available at
www.innerchildpress.com

Inner Child Press Anthologies

Now Available at
www.innerchildpress.com

Inner Child Press Anthologies

Inner Child Press International presents

A Love Anthology 2019

The Love Poets

Now Available

www.worldhealingworldpeacepoetry.com

Inner Child Press Anthologies

Now Available

www.worldhealingworldpeacepoetry.com

Inner Child Press Anthologies

Now Available

www.worldhealingworldpeacepoetry.com

Inner Child Press Anthologies

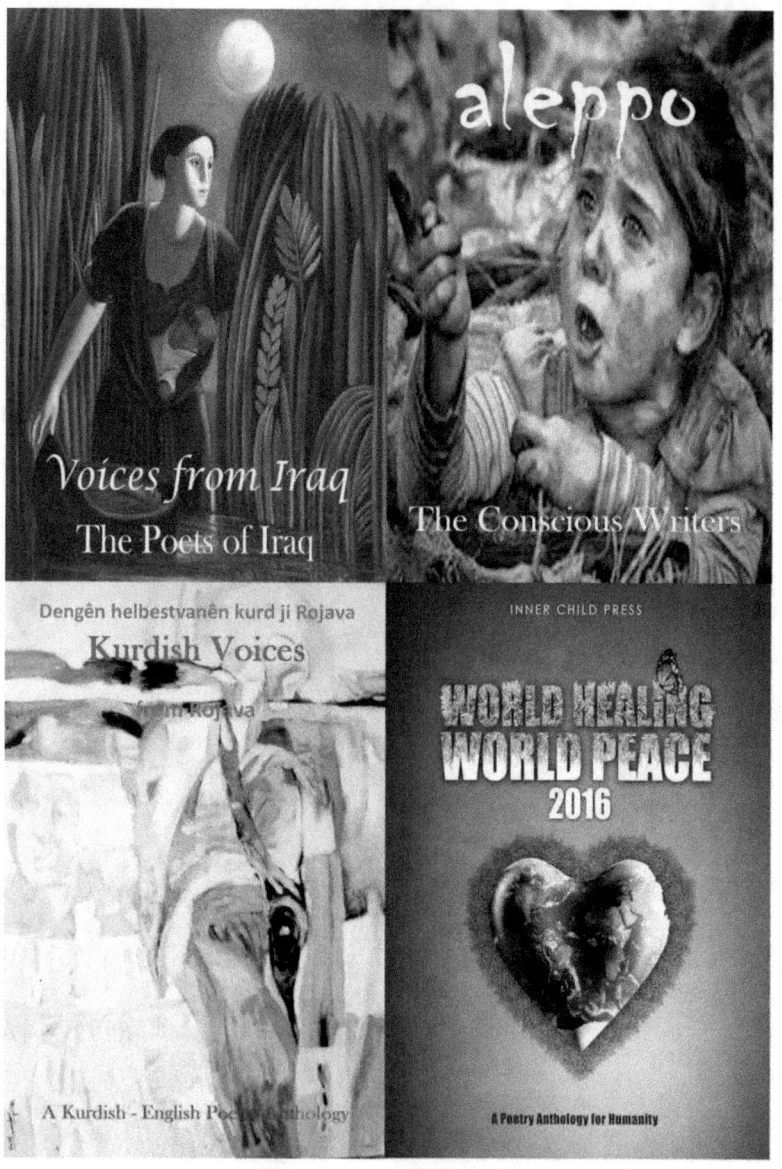

Now Available

www.innerchildpress.com/anthologies

Inner Child Press Anthologies

Now Available

www.innerchildpress.com/anthologies

Inner Child Press Anthologies

Now Available

www.innerchildpress.com/anthologies

Inner Child Press Anthologies

Now Available

www.innerchildpress.com/anthologies

Inner Child Press Anthologies

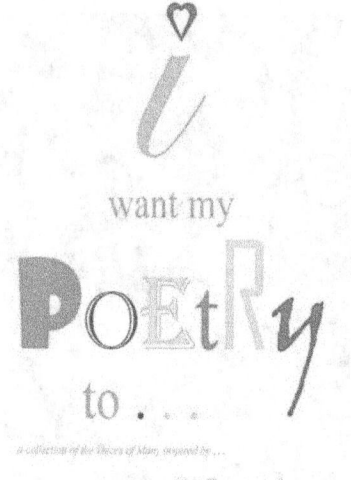

Now Available

www.innerchildpress.com/anthologies

Inner Child Press Anthologies

Now Available

www.innerchildpress.com/the-year-of-the-poet

Inner Child Press Anthologies

Now Available

www.innerchildpress.com/the-year-of-the-poet

Inner Child Press Anthologies

Now Available

www.innerchildpress.com/the-year-of-the-poet

Inner Child Press Anthologies

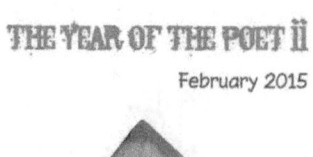

Now Available

www.innerchildpress.com/the-year-of-the-poet

Inner Child Press Anthologies

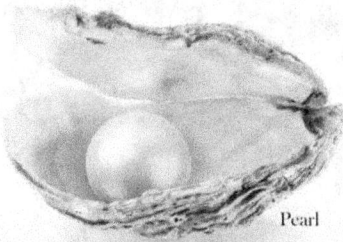
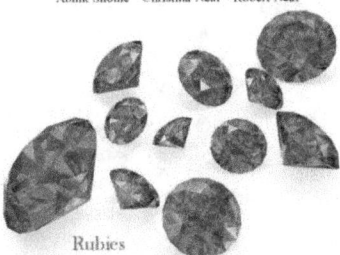
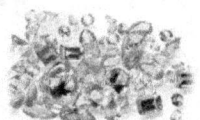

Now Available

www.innerchildpress.com/the-year-of-the-poet

Inner Child Press Anthologies

Now Available

www.innerchildpress.com/the-year-of-the-poet

Now Available

www.innerchildpress.com/the-year-of-the-poet

Inner Child Press Anthologies

Now Available

www.innerchildpress.com/the-year-of-the-poet

Inner Child Press Anthologies

Now Available

www.innerchildpress.com/the-year-of-the-poet

Inner Child Press Anthologies

Now Available

www.innerchildpress.com/the-year-of-the-poet

Inner Child Press Anthologies

Now Available

www.innerchildpress.com/the-year-of-the-poet

Inner Child Press Anthologies

The Year of the Poet IV
September 2017

Featured Poets
Martina Reisz Newberry
Ameer Nassir
Christine Fulco Neal
Robert Neal

The Elm Tree

The Poetry Posse 2017

Gail Weston Shazor * Caroline Nazareno * Bismay Mohanty
Teresa E. Gallion * Anna Jakubczak Vel Ratty Adalan
Joe DaVerbal Minddancer * Shareef Abdur – Rasheed
Albert Carrasco * Kimberly Burnham * Elizabeth Castillo
Hülya N. Yılmaz * Faleeha Hassan * Jackie Davis Allen
Jen Walls * Nizar Sartawi * William S. Peters, Sr.

The Year of the Poet IV
October 2017

Featured Poets
Ahmed Abu Saleem
Nedal Al-Qaeim
Sadeddin Shahin

The Black Walnut Tree

The Poetry Posse 2017

Gail Weston Shazor * Caroline Nazareno * Bismay Mohanty
Teresa E. Gallion * Anna Jakubczak Vel Ratty Adalan
Joe DaVerbal Minddancer * Shareef Abdur – Rasheed
Albert Carrasco * Kimberly Burnham * Elizabeth Castillo
Hülya N. Yılmaz * Faleeha Hassan * Jackie Davis Allen
Jen Walls * Nizar Sartawi * William S. Peters, Sr.

The Year of the Poet IV
November 2017

Featured Poets
Kay Peters
Alfreda D. Ghee
Gabriella Garofalo
Rosemary Cappello

The Tree of Life

The Poetry Posse 2017

Gail Weston Shazor * Caroline Nazareno * Bismay Mohanty
Teresa E. Gallion * Anna Jakubczak Vel Ratty Adalan
Joe DaVerbal Minddancer * Shareef Abdur – Rasheed
Albert Carrasco * Kimberly Burnham * Elizabeth Castillo
Hülya N. Yılmaz * Faleeha Hassan * Jackie Davis Allen
Jen Walls * Nizar Sartawi * William S. Peters, Sr.

The Year of the Poet IV
December 2017

Featured Poets
Justice Clarke
Mariel M. Pabroa
Kiley Brown

The Fig Tree

The Poetry Posse 2017

Gail Weston Shazor * Caroline Nazareno * Bismay Mohanty
Teresa E. Gallion * Anna Jakubczak Vel Ratty Adalan
Joe DaVerbal Minddancer * Shareef Abdur – Rasheed
Albert Carrasco * Kimberly Burnham * Elizabeth Castillo
Hülya N. Yılmaz * Faleeha Hassan * Jackie Davis Allen
Jen Walls * Nizar Sartawi * William S. Peters, Sr.

Now Available

www.innerchildpress.com/the-year-of-the-poet

Inner Child Press Anthologies

Now Available

www.innerchildpress.com/the-year-of-the-poet

Inner Child Press Anthologies

Now Available

www.innerchildpress.com/the-year-of-the-poet

Now Available

www.innerchildpress.com/the-year-of-the-poet

Inner Child Press Anthologies

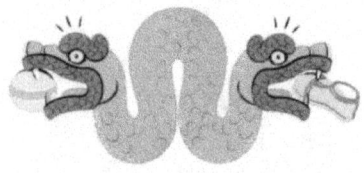

Now Available

www.innerchildpress.com/the-year-of-the-poet

Inner Child Press Anthologies

Now Available

www.innerchildpress.com/the-year-of-the-poet

Inner Child Press Anthologies

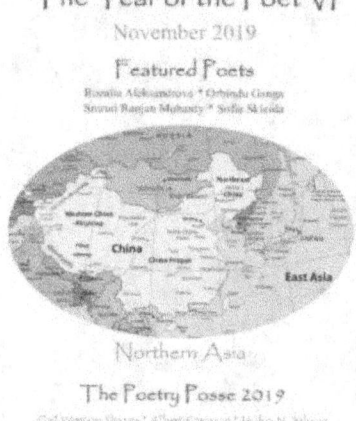

Now Available

www.innerchildpress.com/the-year-of-the-poet

Inner Child Press Anthologies

Now Available

www.innerchildpress.com/the-year-of-the-poet

Inner Child Press Anthologies

Now Available

www.innerchildpress.com/the-year-of-the-poet

Inner Child Press Anthologies

The Year of the Poet VII
September 2020

Featured Poets
Barâ Anis Al-Jubi • Soiknowicz Stefania
Dr. Brajesh Kumar Gupta • Urtnİ Najjarı

Mikhail Sergeyevich Gorbachev ~ 1990

The Year of Peace
Celebrating past Nobel Peace Prize Recipients

The Poetry Posse 2020
Gail Weston Shazor • Albert Carasco • Hülya N. Yılmaz
Jackie Davis Allen • Caroline Nazareno • Eliza Segiet
Alicja Maria Kuberska • Teresa E. Gallion • Joe Paire
Kimberly Burnham • Shareef Abdur – Rasheed
Ashok K. Bhargava • Elizabeth Castillo • Swapna Behera
Tezmin Ition Tsai • William S. Peters, Jr.

The Year of the Poet VII
October 2020

Featured Poets
Mutawaf A. Shaheed • Galina Italyanskaya
Nadeem Fraz • Avril Tanya Meallem

Kim Dae-jung ~ 2000

The Year of Peace
Celebrating past Nobel Peace Prize Recipients

The Poetry Posse 2020
Gail Weston Shazor • Albert Carasco • Hülya N. Yılmaz
Jackie Davis Allen • Caroline Nazareno • Eliza Segiet
Alicja Maria Kuberska • Teresa E. Gallion • Joe Paire
Kimberly Burnham • Shareef Abdur – Rasheed
Ashok K. Bhargava • Elizabeth Castillo • Swapna Behera
Tezmin Ition Tsai • William S. Peters, Jr.

The Year of the Poet VII
November 2020

Featured Poets
Elisa Mascia • Sue Lindenberg McClelland
Hatif Janabi • Ivan Gacina

Liu Xiaobo ~ 2010

The Year of Peace
Celebrating past Nobel Peace Prize Recipients

The Poetry Posse 2020
Gail Weston Shazor • Albert Carasco • Hülya N. Yılmaz
Jackie Davis Allen • Caroline Nazareno • Eliza Segiet
Alicja Maria Kuberska • Teresa E. Gallion • Joe Paire
Kimberly Burnham • Shareef Abdur – Rasheed
Ashok K. Bhargava • Elizabeth Castillo • Swapna Behera
Tezmin Ition Tsai • William S. Peters, Jr.

The Year of the Poet VII
December 2020

Featured Poets
Ratan Ghosh • Ibtisam Ibrahim Al-Asady
Brindha Vinodh • Selma Kopic

Abiy Ahmed Ali ~ 2019

The Year of Peace
Celebrating past Nobel Peace Prize Recipients

The Poetry Posse 2020
Gail Weston Shazor • Albert Carasco • Hülya N. Yılmaz
Jackie Davis Allen • Caroline Nazareno • Eliza Segiet
Alicja Maria Kuberska • Teresa E. Gallion • Joe Paire
Kimberly Burnham • Shareef Abdur – Rasheed
Ashok K. Bhargava • Elizabeth Castillo • Swapna Behera
Tezmin Ition Tsai • William S. Peters, Jr.

Now Available

www.innerchildpress.com/the-year-of-the-poet

and there is much, much more !

visit . . .

www.innerchildpress.com/anthologies-sales-special.php

Also check out our Authors and all the wonderful Books Available at :

www.innerchildpress.com/authors-pages

World Healing World Peace 2020

Poets for Humanity

Now Available

www.worldhealingworldpeacepoetry.com

Now Available

www.worldhealingworldpeacepoetry.com

World Healing World Peace
2012, 2014, 2016, 2018, 2020

Now Available

www.worldhealingworldpeacepoetry.com

Inner Child Press International

building bridges of cultural understanding

Meet the Board of Directors

William S. Peters, Sr.
Chair Person
Founder
Inner Child Enterprises
Inner Child Press

Hülya N Yılmaz
Director
Editing Services
Co-Chair Person

Fahredin B. Shehu
Director
Cultural Affairs

Elizabeth E. Castillo
Director
Recording Secretary

De'Andre Hawthorne
Director
Performance Poetry

Gail Weston Shazor
Director
Anthologies

Kimberly Burnham
Director
Cultural Ambassador
Pacific Northwest
USA

Ashok K. Bhargava
Director
WINAwards

Deborah Smart
Director
Publicity
Marketing

www.innerchildpress.com

Inner Child Press International

'building bridges of cultural understanding'

Meet our Cultural Ambassadors

Fahredin Shehu
Director of Cultural

Faleha Hassan
Iraq – USA

Elizabeth E. Castillo
Philippines

Antoinette Coleman
Chicago
Midwest USA

Ananda Nepali
Nepal – Tibet
Northern India

Kimberly Burnham
Pacific Northwest
USA

Alicja Kuberska
Poland
Eastern Europe

Swapna Behera
India
Southeast Asia

Kolade O. Freedom
Nigeria
West Africa

Monsif Beroual
Morocco
Northern Africa

Ashok K. Bhargava
Canada

Tzemin Ition Tsai
Republic of China
Greater China

Alicia M. Ramirez
Mexico
Central America

Christena AV Williams
Jamaica
Caribbean

Louise Hudon
Eastern Canada

Aziz Mountassir
Morocco
Northern Africa

Shareef Abdur-Rasheed
Southeastern USA

Laure Charazac
France
Western Europe

Mohammad Ikbal Harb
Lebanon
Middle East

Mohamed Abdel
Aziz Shmeis
Egypt
Middle East

Hilary Mainga
Kenya
Eastern Africa

Josephus R. Johnson
Liberia

www.innerchildpress.com

This Anthological Publication
is underwritten solely by

Inner Child Press International

Inner Child Press is a Publishing Company Founded and Operated by Writers. Our personal publishing experiences provides us an intimate understanding of the sometimes daunting challenges Writers, New and Seasoned may face in the Business of Publishing and Marketing their Creative "Written Work".

For more Information

Inner Child Press International

www.innerchildpress.com

'building bridges of cultural understanding'
202 Wiltree Court, State College, Pennsylvania 16801

~ fini ~